BLACK ANGELS

Robert Walicki

Six Gallery Press

BLACK ANGELS © 2018 by Robert Walicki
Published by Six Gallery Press
ISBN: 978-1-989305-00-3
Cover & author photos by Rebecca Clever
First Printing, January 2019

Contents

The Watchers

What The Light Wants   11
Cutfish   14
A Certain Stillness   15
Unseen   17
His Clothes   18
Trying It On   20
Snowfall   22
Enough   24
New Moon   26
Anesthesia   29
The Way Back   31

The Fallen

The Boy   39
The Truth   41
What they don't tell you   43
B-Boy As Andromeda   44
Boy as Girl in Orange Tank Top / How to Eat a Nectarine   46
The Message   48
Collision   50
What I Learned Watching Robert Smith   52
Tattoo   54
B-Boy Meets Future Self   56
Rain   58
Icarus   59

Black Angels

Army/Navy   63
The Crossing   65
Afraid   67
Real Men   69
Running Storm Pipe Under a Bridge Near Akron, 1997   71
Black Angel   73
Underground   76
Tits on a Boy   78
Dmitri   79
Mario Lemieux   80
The Mercy   82
Writing Political Poems at the Squirrel Hill Cafe   85
Work of Hands   87

Beautifully Broken

Reading Between the Lines of an Email to Laurel Garden Apartments, Trying to Get My Security Deposit Back   91
When Your Sister Calls to Tell You She Wrecked the Car on Halloween or How She Became Medusa   93
Top Ten Reasons You Leave Your Sick Kids At Their Grandmother's While Going Black Friday Shopping   95
Still Falling   97
The Moment   98
Visitation   100
Love Locks   102
Pest Control   104
The Climbers   106
1st Coat   108
Spooky Pizza Friday   110
The List   113

for V

BLACK ANGELS

The Watchers

Observe and see how (in the winter) all the trees seem as though they had withered and shed all their leaves...

The Book of Enoch, tr. R.H. Charles

What the Light Wants

Not the tall branches above me rocking and breaking.

Not the dead branches over tree lines too high to touch.

We walk over the grass,

soft blades falling.

The spot we pick is at the edge of the field.

When the wind blows, the rows of pines drop

and brush needles past our faces,

hitting our backs, landing silently around us.

Jan hands me the shovel.

I can feel the slight give of earth when I bear down.

The pole would be first, to support his back,

then clothes for the scarecrow,

my father's flannel,

madras squares quilted and blurred.

I hold his shirt up

and the suddenness comes back,

the rained over windows

and mud slick hill,

running away from shut doors.

In my father's room there was a lack of air.

When he breathed through the tube

my mother would praise him.

Now, I'm sliding on his pants—

wool shirt over wood pole arms,

my sister watching, hands on her hips.

She doesn't know I'm building a man,

stuffing him with dead things—

hay on a stacked pile, loose shoots of grass

cut to exactness.

I have to leave him here,

long stems and thistle.

The crows take pieces of him off with their beaks.

A few tangled lengths cling

to the seat of a tractor.

There are parts of him everywhere.

Cutfish

Down the bank where the fish gills   chip bags   plastic drift

into wet   I told my father   I caught a fish but didn't

want blood   to think of the hook

metal barb into jaw   fish

sucking air   red water   burning

pooled darker as he bled   I let him go

cut the line   left the metal inside

his fish flesh   too wet   it smelled   I was

too young   my hands   slipped

he swam   into the deep   half dead

it wasn't   my fault   I told my father

I caught a fish   sat as my father lay half dead

my hand slipped off   his arm

too wet from the sweat   he smelled

of antiseptic   his flesh   I was

too young   they cut the line   before we got there

the next day   I let him go   burning   he was

sucking air   red water   pooled darker as he bled

through bandages   on his chest   I told my father

I caught a fish   but didn't

A Certain Stillness

The stillness of the trees before the wind came

and no rain, but a dampness.

The air held it

and leaves, turned up at the edges

like thousands of drinking cups

and both hands to hold them, bare feet

walking up the carpet to him at midnight

and maybe you drip or spill a little on his hands

as he gets up slightly from the bed

to thank you and take the cup

coughing and shaking behind doors

rocking the cage of his breath, what

your mother has learned to sleep through.

Time, flaking paint on the backyard shed

crumbling driveway and high grasses becoming weeds

garbage leaning against the house, overflowing

everything

let go

and when the wind comes, it moves the branches

and some water spills, so it seems like it's raining.

Unseen

For answers, reach down into the small of your father's underwear drawer

for the meaning of slick skin, the pages of screaming bodies, red and desperate

in their hunger. Add a woman in a tiara and mink stole. Nothing

else. Bend her body into the shape of a question mark and leave her there,

all red-mouthed and knees, because nothing says love like hard floors and rooms

without windows, like walls the color of sickness. There are a hundred more

pages like this. But listen, do you know you're dreaming this and falling out

of your body, the air falling too, and the snow, erasing the memory of tire tracks,

the path to the hospital, last shot of you frozen, the live wire of your hair,

explosion of your mouth, heart attack, crash cart, EKG machine turned off.

The relatives, coming in waves, crash of bodies, sobbing hugs, and you,

trapped in a last scream, like these couples, eyes closed over the shock

of each page turning, the miles of blank bodies. All those places

your hands have seen.

His Clothes

Afterwards, there was so much
left, his dress shirt and brown slacks

knotted in a soft embrace,
the caved in chest of a jacket,

twang of a hanger on a metal rod,
an IV cart left behind in haste.

My mother untangled their arms
and legs, folded them in halves,

packed them in the bag they gave.
The bed was already made.

The meds on the nightstand
with one refill left. The kindness

of two coupons given, free meals
at the cafeteria from the nurses'

station. They sent us to the correct
elevator, asked if we had

everything, if the room was clear.

His nurse, walking back to his

room before the door slid closed,

just wanted to make one more

sweep. What I remember most

though were her shoes,

pristine white, with those Velcro strips

that ripped when she walked.

The wedge of a heel

rubbed uneven, how she went back again

to his room to see, because she didn't

believe, her own wrinkled palm

pressed against his bed,

smoothing those new sheets down.

Trying It On

I fist the small holes

where the arms go, hard

and crisp. Stiff, starched shirts

of my father's. I try them on alone.

It's weeks after his wake,

that night my cousin scoured my aunt's

pantry for more vodka, cold chicken and crackers,

asking me if I knew who I wanted to be.

He's drunk, I know, and eating

with his mouth open, but he stares at me

as if he knows something I don't.

The first time I went in, no one was home.

I opened my father's closet and peeled off

one of his shirts, *teal*—not my color,

but long enough to fit, its itch rubbing

against my chest, big as a secret and smelling

of men's cologne, the button at the top

tight around my neck. His scared son

trying on a pale shirt he left

behind, still keeping

its creased shape.

I slid myself into his pale, green arms,

what held on to his body.

Snowfall

"Tell me about the last time you saw your father,"
my therapist said. *He wasn't speaking,*

but eating, I said. *I can't go back,*
to the space before there were words

that meant something. His mouth was moving,
chewing something. He was hungry

and getting seconds,
hot waffles and crisp, sizzling bacon

at The Holy Name Breakfast.
I remember windows and the sun's blindness,

because of snow, the sounds of scraping
on windshields, his spinning tires,

a phone call, and the heart attack. *I was safe,*
I said, inside, listening to tires slicing

the road in halves. The ambulance approaching
slow, with the lights turned off,

There were no words for this yet.

What do you want from me?

I remember the snow, I said. *It was steady,* overwhelming in its beauty.

Enough

The next day, the lights are still on from the night before,

or it's sunny, coming home from church dressed in black,

and someone reaches for the remote, or someone asks her,

How are the children? and it's Sunday, so,

There's gotta be a football game on, and, *Honey, how are you...really?*

Behind, her the door swings and slams the wind.

The room fills with relatives and the fan swings on its axis.

The clip-on angel sways from the chain end.

And when the kitchen door closes,

she slips away, tilts her head back, blinks fifteen times,

whatever it takes,

to peel back the layers

of foil, make sure everyone has enough.

Day passes, and someone scores, and someone yells at the TV,

and someone says, *Leave the food out!*

because someone might want it.

And the men will go off to play cards till 3 a.m.,

and the women will talk outside.

If there is a garden, or a veranda to look at,

I don't remember.

No one sleeps.

But every so often, someone gets up,

like on a shift or doing the rounds

for security, and they might open the fridge and then shut it,

going back to the food that's been left out

to pick at it.

I don't why it was,

how every time,

everyone seemed so hungry,

how none of us could get enough.

New Moon

Tonight, when my mother sees it,

it's hovering through a beam of stars,

the full moon, bald in its harshness,

cracked, like her ceiling's plaster

from the roof leaks I never fixed.

"Did you see how big this is?" she asks,

but I'm on my cell, driving under its spotlight,

a moon so huge, so insistent on illumination,

going home through a blindness I can't name.

The weather at 11 mentions positions,

how the tides and the winds will affect things

in countries far away from her.

But tomorrow will bring her another purpose,

yesterday's coffee, hot again, and the cable truck

hauling optical fibers, laying out their spiderwork of lines,

the 500 channels she can't live without. I'm leaving

my mother home again, to a remote control that works,

the blue glow of her shows, masses in Rome

or the elimination round of a cooking program.
Whoever can make the avocado look sexy gets to stay.
She's happy now, to never fall in love

with ingredients, to learn the advice she'll never take.
Sunday dinners, when she'd wash fettuccine like laundry,
cook it scalding hot, till it's stiff,

unravel rubber lengths stuck to the bottoms of pots.
But dinner is a mother I can't bear to judge.
What can I do but swallow,

ask for more meatballs hard as craters, one more
dollop of sauce? Because someday the phone will stop ringing.
Someday no one will call my name.

At home, the Discovery Channel is talking about moons,
artists' renditions of chalky white devastation, rivers
filled with nothing but memory, tide and shore,

the years of weathering, becoming basin, shell.
They are emptying her car out on the interstate after the crash,
shrapnel of coins in gravel, strewn clothes. "I'm okay," she says,

calling me for a ride home. That's how it is sometimes.

To be loved is to be held down by something you can't see,

the sleeping arm of a lover, or the mother

who needed a ride, but you were paralyzed with exhaustion.

Sometimes the only thing the day can offer you is sleep,

a moon you wouldn't think twice about,

that will be there tomorrow and the next, doing its bright purpose,

inevitable as a phone call or gravity, pulling

the living close to it, never letting them go.

Anesthesia

Hemp rope muscles twist,

tie themselves with little effort.

Just sitting here at Conley's

is enough to tighten the knot.

Even after last call, doors locked,

the ghost of his sweat haunts

this oak, worn bar top where he rested

his denim arm. A few bills

earned him this medicine,

amber-tinged sour mash,

anything cheap, domestic,

whatever was on tap.

Clank of dirty glassware,

laughter. Ripped leather

bar stools and piss troughs

at his feet. At eight, I remember

how my grandfather's breath

took my breath away. I wrecked

my BMX in thick hollows while he fell

daily, in the made-up dust

of B movie Westerns. John Wayne,

bar fights, gunfire. I poured Pabst

Blue Ribbon in baby cups for him

like my grandmother told me to,

spillproof plastic for his shaking hands.

Every time he closed his eyes,

he went somewhere. Ghost towns,

the bar at the end of the street.

I pushed the drapes back, left his bedroom

lights on so he could find his way back home.

The Way Back

1

Somewhere, there is a way back in,

through a word like

recollect

or *lattice*.

Somewhere, the way through is

the path to the house,

where your feet disappear

in the mud sucked earth,

where ground turns to water—

call it a river.

You were young.

2

The way grass has grown high.

The way ash from the fire nurtures soil.

3

Today, I am on the hill where the house was.

I draw the floor plan in the air

with my finger,

and the white door swings open.

The room, opening to waves,

deep swirls of brown paneling,

rippled and pulled from the wall.

The ceiling's cumulus plaster

cracking, the big house settling.

The built-ins still packed

with porcelain ducks and singing angels.

And I'm trying to remember that wall,

my grandmother's house

on a Saturday,

my mother listening to jazz.

Her friends had dates,

took her brushes,

never painted before.

But suddenly,

the wall was filled with hemlocks

and deer drank from streams,

walking out of the wall

down the street past me,

and somewhere past me

there was water,

a stream.

Somewhere there was a way back in.

The kitchen windows steaming from heat,

a blurry view of the Allegheny,

grey barges like grave markers pulling steel.

Her mother at the stove,

back turned,

disappearing into the mist.

4

I am downstairs where the last of her things needs boxed up.

In the photograph I ask to keep, nothing moves.

It is 1933 and she is standing in a bread line.

It could have been minutes or hours.

No one owns a watch.

Time is the length of space

between each of her footsteps.

The time it takes to get inside

before they run out.

I am trying to remember the last time

I touched her.

I hold the photograph up to the light.

My thumb touches her face

but she doesn't notice.

The distance is clear

but no one can see past it.

5

The way a door shuts on its own.

The way the wind lets go of my hand.

6

When I stepped back outside, and the house disappeared.

7

In a room she won't remember,

I sit on the edge of her bed.

We are somewhere and the light is coming through the open blinds,

the thin slats splintering air.

And I am waiting until you open your eyes

to tell you it is morning.

The Fallen

It was snowing

And it was going to snow.

The blackbird sat

In the cedar-limbs.

Wallace Stevens

The Boy

Today when the neighbor boys are beating the bejeezus

out of the kid next door, it's because of his clothes

and the way he walks. I hear the garbage truck.

Last time they forgot two bags,

now I'm watching his collar pulled,

books dropped and tripped,

jaws crushing

coffee grounds, empty egg cartons,

ripped shirt, bloody nose.

The arms push it further.

Next house, there's a couch

without springs and some old computers,

and he is lying on the sidewalk where they left him.

The other boys will part ways,

go home

or out to eat,

because it's Friday.

And two more of them will walk together

because they are friends,

still laughing about it down the street.

What I saw taught me how to stand by,

how to say nothing. It was cold, bright,

the kind of light that catches a window

of a neighbor's car door when it opens,

and for a moment, you can't see anything.

The Truth

We pulled the wings off flies and bugs

just to watch them struggle. We didn't

look at ourselves as cruel, our hands full.

Call it curiosity.

We couldn't hurt anything unless we were dared

to. *Hit that bird. Hit that snake*

slithering through grass,

or glistening on the bank.

The river's terse edge, rocks, water,

the places I was afraid to cross or come close to.

Someone always was struck with the urge to push you over

into the deep end—the unsafe waves,

caved in hills, our bikes peering over

like small animals looking down,

ignoring popped chains, stitches, our mother's screams

standing on porches or leaning out of windows,

still haggardly pretty and we, too young to see

the truth we were getting close to,

like the bodies of beetles, those mosquitoes

I kept in the open air grave under my bed,

specks of matter intangible as dust,

so fragile that when you touch them for the first time,

some of them would stay there, unable to move,

others flying off as if wakened by your touch.

What they don't tell you

about the shame of locked bathrooms,

that being Catholic had everything to do with the body.

Jesus is watching you, my mother would say,

and I thought about the empty house and the white noise of trees,

sheets, anything to drown the sound of discovery.

My hand, a beating wing, desolate field,

sweaty race of skin, eyes closed to the burning

soft exhaustion, and afterwards, the paper towels.

When I heard their voices I knew the door had opened,

that downstairs, coats were coming off, and there was laughter,

the wet heat from takeout bags reaching me.

Upstairs, I put on heavy clothes because it was winter.

Because my mother called my name, I went downstairs

to eat with them.

B-Boy As Andromeda

It's easy to dream on your back,

a room spinning under your body

to the thumps of deep tracks,

rap and scratch beat breaking your body

before you were broken.

Ten years before your back would shatter

into unanswered questions,

before the world of hard hat and ladder

descended on you like a downpour,

sent you underground to your first live sewer.

Before you learned darkness, you learned to moonwalk,

melting into cymbal and drum machine, your skin

a silk sail catching air, swish

of ocean from your neon legs.

Break dancing in a tenement basement,

you learn what it means for a boy to burn,

become electric under the voodoo shudder

of crushed grooves, undressing to song

after song that whispered your name,

blue as a constellation, though the bedroom stars

you dreamed under for so long were already dying.

Boy as Girl in Orange Tank Top / How to Eat a Nectarine

You'll need fingernails like a girl's

to push down with, dig deep into skin,

pull off the shredded pieces of an orange tank top,

long legs to stand with, until a bedroom mirror

becomes a baseball field. That day they saw you,

said, *Who's that ugly girl?* and something unraveled.

His fists, the knife, torn locks of hair from your head.

Girl in mud. Girl with the lisp. Pretty lips. Boy/

girl, be careful. Become a boy.

Play nice. Learn war

and learn to break his little soldier arms.

Throw him off the sofa cliff.

Make those noises with your mouth again,

for explosions. Girl, become a boy.

Learn to wrestle, pull dogs' tails,

hide your no-boy muscles under longish shirts.

Pick fights. Learn to spit. Dig deep.

Bite down and swallow.

The Message

At ten, before any of us knew anything,

we staged protests in the form of headstands,

learning about racial equality in a Stanton Heights basement.

I heard *The Message* from Grandmaster Flash, breakdancing

on a piece of leftover linoleum, while the record skipped

a beat, the needle digging a groove—

we made our backs slick, rubbing oil on floors to make

us spin faster, while kids starved and drive-by shootings happened,

to a beat our bodies moved to.

Shaking in our parachute pants as if

on fire, electric as Michael Jackson moonwalking for the first time.

We wanted to glide over broken asphalt, our high-tops scuffing

up air like water before anything mattered.

Before anyone could tell by looking that I was white and my friend was black.

Before that old guy got pulled out of his car at the top of my mother's street,

beaten and robbed, before sirens and glass breaking,

the sounds of kids running at night. Before my mother told me that it

wasn't safe to walk and I should look in the mirror because I'd know why.

Because years later it was me on a ladder painting walls in my mother's

house when the power went dead because Richard Poplawski (who was white)

shot three police officers less than a mile from her house.

Before the twelve-year-old Italian kid from down the street stole mail from people's boxes, got arrested, then said it was my idea.

Because my eighth grade teacher (a nun) asked me why I listen

to that music and *Don't you know you're white?*

Because I should walk fast when alone or if it's dark,

especially in mall parking lots and questionable neighborhoods, because

anything can happen and *Don't you watch the news?*

Because every time I should, I hear that music. I see kids standing on a corner

and a beat seeks me out for a body to move with.

My hand first, a wave moving through, my feet and legs swept

away by this song, these words, this whoever I was, becoming.

Collision

I've come again and again to this place,

no address or name, past the flashing street lights

and the crematorium on the left.

It's summer, but I'm here for the inside—

black walls, shot out windows, the dance floor

a wasteland of missing tiles and spit,

beer cans, burnt cigs. There's no disco

ball here, just the backs of heads,

teenage sweat, tattoos bursting from ripped denim.

I wait to move in the purple light

for a band I've never heard of,

primal scream of guitars tearing me open

like the poems I haven't read yet.

What I know about grief

I swallow from a can I smuggled in

from the parking lot, all of us sad kids staggering

toward the stage, spinning heads into elbows.

Learning closeness

by slamming our bodies into each other.

Everything that we wanted and wanted to be,

lost in the smoke-thick dark, in bathrooms making out,

by stages under lights, shaking

like freight trains jumping the tracks,

screaming in the dark.

What I know of love, I learn in this collision,

holding my ears, still burning

from guitar fire, and what it means to be alive.

After the show, a glimpse from the back room,

the band, still stoned, the air a sweet cloud

that hangs like indecision, the drummer,

turning to me, blowing toward my face,

tiny butt in his hand becoming ash,

then wisp of smoke, then nothing.

What I Learned Watching Robert Smith

In 1994, when Robert Smith enters your bedroom,

you play it cool. Even if he's scotch taped to the walls,

underworld clown from your teenage hell, *that weirdo*

your grandmother called him.

In this shot his hair is electric, crazed with shock,

a wind tunnel of Aqua Net, that red lipped boy from Blackpool.

Soon, your mother will worry about you,

your father, who hopes the freak phase passes,

will listen by the door while you mainline

MTV into your eardrums. New Order, the Smiths,

and more sissy music like this. Before your last day of senior year,

you will leave the house under cover of darkness.

So much will depend on how soft the front door closes,

if that Ford Fiesta will be there waiting, with 200 miles

between you and Cleveland. One busted transmission

and five tickets to see the Cure, Robert Smith,

pole up his tortured ass, bolted down to that stage.

Dear beautiful turnstile. Dear mime left out in the rain,

I want to drive into the wreck of those screaming guitars,

listen to him belt out Close to Me and Pictures of You,

the mic so close he could kiss it, sing out his British

heartbreak and tear up my 18 years as if they were nothing,

searchlights flooding the stage, my hands over my ears,

trying to hold so much in.

Tattoo

For it to happen, a stranger's hand needs to touch you,

gloves thinner than air, arms brushing breasts and pecs,

fields of skin becoming dragons or two snakes biting the shit

out of each other's tails, in an endless circle of scar and color.

I can afford more than black and white. I still have a job.

My sister's car hasn't smacked a pole yet.

I thought I'd never want to do this, too afraid of superheroes

and Betty Boop at 80. Jody says, *It's a big decision,*

and she has enough holes in her face to make me believe her.

But aren't we already full of it, of emptiness? *Maybe a skull,* I say.

Something tough. Have anything with thorns? In Artisan, the parlor

in Garfield, tattooed goths sip coffee, wait their turn. I order a latte,

the opposite of reckless, a part of me already raw,

already burning red. Drink almost finished and my phone is shaking

from texts, Nina's secret cutting again. I don't know what to say to her mother but *Sorry. If you need anything.* And now I'm holding the door for the girl

with blue hair who's done this before, upper body, a flutter of fish

scales, thorns wrapped around a wrist. She sits down for the burning needle.

Everyone here is waiting to carve beauty into their bodies, but I couldn't

tell the story again. Dear body, I'll do anything, just

name it—room inside a forest, boy inside a bird's mouth,

dragon fire, screaming cars on a hill, the winter of no breath,

snowfall, slow tires, father's frozen scream

inside a scream inside a scream.

Jody shows me catalogs of pics, everything she can do to skin,

and now I want the raven, wings black and reaching past my shoulders,

but I'm afraid of flying. I leave the ghost in me there,

pale skin scrubbed within seconds of red.

My almost body, my what did you do to yourself body,

and walk out, let the door close into a smear of hands,

smear of sunlight, smear of me on glass,

still inside, disappearing into the black.

B-Boy Meets Future Self

The first time your body broke was to sound.

Years before your back shattered its vertebrae

like oyster shells, the ER doctor looking at you

for signs from a flashlight, his nearsightedness

mistaken for mystic fog. Concussion symptoms

ignored because dirty socks and muddy steel toe

boots sit beside this bed. When they wheel you in for MRIs

and ask about music to play in the echo chamber,

say rap, say bebop.

Become small enough to fit in the half shell,

paper gown floating above your body to the whirls and clicks.

Remember kitchen floors where you learned to backspin,

glide Nikes over tiles as if you were weightless.

While they check for brokenness, think of movement,

how cuts from Grandmaster Flash and Run-DMC

on cassette can act as weapons if bullied.

How a needle on an LP or in an arm

can mark you for instinct, trading a head spin

for feeling in your legs, grateful to be moving again.

After six months, they will want you back in the same

muddy hole, work ethic mistaken for a sense of rhythm.

Rain

for Prince

In his king's robe made out stars, he waits,

lifts his river of hair to stare at us,

scream his beautiful mess of torture,

reach a slow hand down to touch strings,

make it rain for the first time.

My sister hid you for months,

snuck listens to *Purple Rain* at night

in safety, muffling your moans with low sound

and headphones, the LP she slipped between a wall

and a bookcase.

But once, no one in the house, I found you,

turned you up, not knowing what it meant

to lay a needle down into a groove,

set the storm inside me spinning.

I was young, what did I know of closed eyes,

a wet mouth, the wing of someone's hand over my body,

what purple rain means when it falls on your skin,

how you never want it to stop.

Icarus

for David Bowie

Wipes the paint off

his porcelain Christ face,

drapes hand me downs,

bolts of silk, florid patterns

on his back. Lifts his lost head

into fog, rock and roll,

flashing lights, cop bright,

identifies the lightness in every step.

The heat in his head spreads,

descends to his shoulders,

melts the wax off his wings,

and he falls.

Black Angels

If you're old enough to read this,

you know what work is.

Phillip Levine

Army/Navy

after Jan Beatty

I am looking for clothes to hide my body in,

canvas pants wrench stiff and a jacket cut like a man,

green leaf camouflage to disappear behind,

cotton duck coveralls for the ditch I'll be in

tomorrow, laying muddy pipe. If you have

enough money, Carhartt can turn you into a man,

coats like chain mail, a puffed out chest

tough as hell for the fight tomorrow

with the general, a contractor who spits in your face,

calls you *bitch* like the rest.

Today, I find a place on Butler called Army/Navy,

heavy curtains, window with a neon sign flashing OPEN

in lipstick red. Inside, a motorcycle boy in chaps,

handlebar mustache, asks if he can help,

says, *We have videos in the back, all persuasions.*
Anything you want.

Gas masks, 15 inch heels, a riding crop, soft
handcuffs with pink puffy feathers,

leather, vinyl body suits, and breast plates with pecs
or tits molded into them.

These empty shells on hangers, this waiting for a body.

And it's enough to make me want those jeans,
that shiny black skin, their slickness. The more and more of it,

whipping someone for the pleasure—

but I'm here for armor. I imagine settling on a bomber,
new metal zipper, brass teeth gleaming.

Leaving it on even though it's 90 out.
Letting everyone see what's happening,

all that sweat running down my skin.

The Crossing

You stand at the mouth of the Mon,

half tuned up on Bud

or Samuel Adams Summer Ale.

Extra bottles stuffed in your pockets meant

for fishing lures or slip shots that clink when you walk.

And you talk for a while, never facing anyone,

undulating flash of river carrying rainbows

and browns away from the car trouble,

the son flunked out, the job you hate.

The key is to get to the other side.

You know this without speaking,

know how to move through tide

by wedging one foot between stones,

their moss covered smoothness,

a void indicating surety, balance.

But you are afraid to hold on to the man in front of you,

afraid of what touch means, so you let that room full

of trees spin on the drunken axis of itself and fall,

cool push of water on your chest, the river,

entering your clothes. Kevin laughs.

This happens every year,

someone steps wrong and falls.

Next time hold on to me, he says,

turning away before you can see his face.

Afraid

You were afraid they could tell by looking

you were *that kind* of man, because of the dead

deer who dove into the front end of your truck

headfirst. *I saw horns*, you said, and they asked, *Why*

didn't you stop for the rack? It was

because you were shaking and your breath left your body

like an apparition. Because you left him there, carried his blood

with you on a dented fender, while plumbers in hard hats joked,

caressed twisted steel like a trophy,

looked at you differently after this,

handed you tools instead of *Hey, get this,*

let you drill holes by yourself in steel roofs,

knees bent, grinder bearing down,

throwing sparks, screaming into air.

Don't say it, or anything.

Your only defense is to cut metal

in skips and burning stars, sharp as the wind chill,

afraid to say the wrong thing,

Beautiful instead of *Cool* and *Good job.*

Like how unwashed denim can save you, stiffen your walk

in the harsh, shrill wind, enough to grab a wrench,

something heavy enough to kill a man or tighten a nut.

Everyone here looking tough without trying,

grabbing their crotches to adjust, spit chew,

stare longer than they should at you,

as if they know, and they do.

Real Men

Say it loud in a huff.

Shoot off their mouths and heavy guns,

drag bloody deer, leave their hearts on the ground.

Real men roll their sleeves up,

a handful of chips, edge of a mouth,

dripping with sauce, give you shit.

Real men screw tool boxes down to floors,

put rocks in your hubcaps, lock you in portajohns, tip them over.

Real men call you *sissy* and *bitch*

quick as a fist bump, a punch in the gut at break,

say, *I thought you'd done this before?*

Water break, gas leak, jackhammer between your balls

in some grandma's basement. Say this breaking is necessary,

flaking concrete, ears and shoulders burning.

So when the ground opens, grab a shovel

and get down on your knees, keep moving as if this is your religion,

your hands, the cuts and blood,

the men standing above you in hard hats laughing.

Every man you've ever met resembles the father you couldn't know.

The father, heavy as the shadows that fall over you,

6 feet of leaning earth, this ditch line, crumbling

into the shape of a body, your body, learning.

Running Storm Pipe Under a Bridge Near Akron, 1997

When the only heat is from the coffee

at 5 a.m. and it's less than 4 degrees outside,

you'll learn to wear enough layers,

or better yet, keep moving.

Some biker dude will laugh, blow frost,

Marlboro smoke in your face.

First day, it's *Hey, rookie* and *Don't look down*.

It's *Lift this* 8 inch, cast iron pipe.

First day, it's *Go down to my truck and get*

my pipe stretcher, and then you'll realize

there's no such thing 4 stories down.

First day, men will want to break you

like they've been broken, their riverbed faces,

grizzled beards twisted like dry rotted wire,

last night's whiskey sweating from dirty skin.

You will nearly lose your finger when the ice forms

on the pipe, straps loosening, metal slamming flesh.

If you can make it past this, there's a Miller Genuine Draft.

There's a welder sitting next to you, buys the first round,

lays his steel hands on your shoulder

like the father who couldn't bear it.

If you can make it past tomorrow,

you'll have to trust the pig iron,

this foot width of rust,

and walk this I-beam, 50 feet of crosscut steel

falling into nothing. There's a strap that holds

your waist, a broken man who leads you.

He'll walk like a free man across 4 inches of steel.

He'll never look back.

Black Angel

Because I refused to listen,

because the words *college* and *textbook*

fell off my body like indifferent rain,

I became a raven.

Or, more accurately, one of those men,

head down, shiny black raincoat,

hands made of mud, digging out some

broken drain. Instead of wings,

ravens like this get stormwater, they get 6

hours of shit filled pipe overflowing,

followed by...

I'm wasn't on the job when the sprinkler

fitter stepped wrong, missed the bar

on the scissor lift, fell 50 feet down.

Because he didn't know

about the no wing policy at jobsites.

Because they issued us free lunch and Budweiser

instead of harness,

canvas straps for our working class lives.
We sat on our hands at the safety meetings,
our invisible wings the only things moving.

I could have left then, but we ravens are short range flyers.
We can spot a quarter on a sidewalk
as if it were a drop of blood 50 feet up.

Because we need the dead as much as the ground does
to fill our hunger, paychecks folded into dirty hands
every Monday like a drug,

so we wouldn't spend everything,
so we would always come back.

General said, *There's a certain type of man*

wants to fit pipe, set shitters, tear down walls,
remove asbestos without a mask.
WebMD said it lies inside the body,

as in dormant, as in 20-30 years,

as in were I holding a bullet and mesothelioma

in the palm of each hand

would it matter which opened first?

I saw the Angel of Death

walk outside a condemned building,

hole in his respirator,

cigarette hanging from his mouth. He was

just going outside for some fresh air

for a moment. *Beautiful day*, he said.

Underground

To break ground means to spit,

make them believe it comes natural,

your Durango strut, smooth jaw, Brillo rough

and cut this frozen earth with pick swings, 7 a.m.

You're 20 and fresh out of art school. Your masterpiece

Mystical Autumn got an A minus,

but now you are the thing you do.

Sweat jeweling off your boy body,

a skinny, jeaned thing, dizzy headed,

but thirsty to push a shovel down

into thick clefts of strata, the harpoon

in your shoulder, burning.

What they don't tell you in school

is that you'll have to touch the snake,

50 feet of coiled steel, rust caked from its eely bath,

its shit journey down some stranger's dark hole.

And when the plumber tells you to pick it up, you do

as you're told, because first years are dirt, fresh meat

primed to be broken, tentacles shaking in your dirty hands

nearly snapping your wrist like a twig.

You never thought you'd be here, riding shotgun

in a plumbing van, its dashboard a landscape

of fast food wrappers, sitting next to Stu or Bull or Jumbo.

Everyone with catcher's mitt faces and cuds of chew.

And that man called your boss with the crooked face,

his fat chest laughing its king of hell laugh,

saying, *This is how you learn*, and *Good job,*

and *Keep moving.*

Tits on a Boy

Because everyone here is older than you,
means it's your job to carry the concrete saw,
the mini jackhammers down the ladder.

The wrench of your back, the quiver of your knees.
Because of thieves, you chain 40 hours of work to rusty I-beams,
the wet saw that numbed your hands,

the hammer drill that kicked you off a 12 foot ladder,
smacked the work ethic out of your wrists.
It's not safe to wear a watch, but you'll know it's over when they tell you it is,

when someone pulls a static radio by its tail
and Led Zeppelin stops playing. No one invites anyone to anything,
but you'll know it's Friday from the plume of exhaust,

the rattling trucks you're meant to follow
to the bar you've never heard of,
sit next to a man who called you *useless as tits on a boy*, laughing.

Keep watching as their faces change with every shot they throw back,
the next beer they buy you. They're smiling.
They've waited their whole lives for this.

Dmitri

Because the top of our awning needed painting and he was available.
Because a friend of a friend recommended him, said he's real thorough,

won't hit you over the head, which meant cheap, which meant he spent
too many years breathing the outer space of a paint can's dizzy fumes.

Because his clothes are a universe of Jackson Pollack splatters,
but I didn't think "artist" the first time I met him.

Because he put his Turner tea carton down to tell me about the time he painted
the Roberto Clemente Bridge underneath without a harness and I believed him.

Because when his face is flecked with semigloss he's oblivious to the off white
burning. Because he'll be done in time for $3 shots at Billy Kay's happy hour.

Because I burned down my 25 year old lungs painting rooms without windows
because I needed money and was young and my lazy prick of a boss said do it.

Because it's the liquor that saves us, shots of Jack being cheaper than anesthesia,
Dmitri's hand shaking when I give him his check. Because when he shakes

off his tarp in the yard, a confetti of paint dust rains down
and he folds the squares perfectly, as if it were ceremony, leaving nothing behind

but this off kilter air, our wet roof still shining.

Mario Lemieux

Mario waits for the puck in a New Kensington living room,

the wall poster action shot above a worn out couch.

A woman bends down to sweep her carpet with a broom—

dog hair, Dorito crumbs, torn receipts. I wait

with tools to be told where the broken sink is.

That was 92, she says. *Their second cup.*

Third period. I was there when he scored the game winner,

banged that puppy right in. I walk past toys, strewn clothes,

a ceiling fan dangling by the wires, and kneel before the porcelain god,

a cracked sink and faucet that screams burning hot water or nothing

at all. When I leave, the new sink shines like a full moon in the dark

of burned out lamps, the unswept dirt of pizza crusts and Legos,

Mario on the wall, looming like a ghost on ice before the shot,

before any goal could save a city. In town, the buildings I pass

fade into a wet blur flecked with rain, the businesses stripped

of names, boarded up glass, soaped up or duct taped.

Nothing open but a bar and a bank, Citizens

flashing alive in neon.

No one here will be scoring anything tonight, except

a little weed, a six pack after work and the game on,

the ice cleaned of its scratches, the cuts made new,

all of our TV's filling our rooms with blue light

to a chorus of screams,

that hunger we don't want to name.

The Mercy

In the row houses of Trafford, there are women
like Michelle, three kids and two-bedroom lean-tos,

cutting hair in the basement for cash. If you know her,
she'll cut you. No exceptions, never advertised.

Everything about cellars like hers are tough.
Deer heads bolted to walls, a carp screaming from a log.

Scissors, the weapons of beauty, jammed in cluttered jars,
the hot pink curling pins like spent shells in a pile.

What is there to do but look
in the mirror, at her rough hands, afraid to say anything

but *Great job* or *Love what you've done to it.*
Ellie slumps in the wash chair, the tough daughter

arguing about dinner in camos. Calloused hands
from playing drums, stuffing deer heads for fun.

She lifts up her bare foot next to me, as if it was natural, asks if any of us want to see the bruises on her leg from the sled.

I wait for you in the man chair, know I couldn't be tougher than any of this,
next to working class wives and their men,

the dead end jobs, clothes at home in the wash. Everyone here is waiting
for the grey to be erased, for their color to go deep.

I meet Don, the husband in the garage with a new deer head.
Tanned it this morning, he says. *6 p.m., you can still smell the glue.*

I'm watching the deer head, the stunned glass eyes,
and this camo guy caressing it with a tenderness that scares me.

In a cut out pic, you show Michelle who you want to be
and you are transformed. Blower growling to life, spewing hot air in your face,

clouds of Aqua Net choking the air with spray.
The ride home after paying her is the quarter tank of hoping

we can make it till payday, the 8 o'clock hunger
filling the backseat with a landscape of plastic bags.

The roast and frozen veg, the unmade
lasagna that'll last us for days.

Between the abandoned strip mall and the auto wreckers,

the sky is a quiet eruption of red, burning sunsets

down in the back of NAPA's parking lot.

Nothing on earth is supposed to look this beautiful,

diffusion of light, empty mouth at this, flash of windshield,

this turning into blindness. I turn up the radio and Bob Seger

growl-screams, *Roll me away, I'm gonna roll me away tonight,*

and now we're two-wheeling it, our hair, dirty wind,

hot chrome between our legs, over these beat up Pittsburgh roads.

When the song ends, I'm still inside my pickup

thinking of the deer head,

the pinned-open mouth, eyes like oceans.

Right before it moves, you'll know it, Don says.

One shot to the heart, before it bleeds out.

I know what you're thinking, man, but this is a mercy.

Key is to find it soon, preserve that look of beauty.

Writing Political Poems at the Squirrel Hill Café

for Jason Irwin

After a few beers we talk honestly, agree we're not good at writing them.

I nod my head instead of saying I remember where I was when it happened,

on a forklift building bingo orders when the first plane hit. Now, a month after

the 2016 election, a physical therapist will yell at me for not trying harder.

I'll lay the $20 copay down for the right to wait for him, watch the intern fix

a broken skeleton on a carpeted floor. Do three sets of ten

on my bad hip, listen to him talk about the mess of healthcare,

how his parents voted for Trump, how he doesn't speak to them anymore.

Drinking here with you, it never occurs to me that nothing

will ever be the same again, just that this is something we have to do, to sit

on these crooked barstools, let the liquor speak for us, warm our aching bones.

It seems like it should snow on a night like this, but maybe the cold's here

just to remind us that we're broken too, that we don't have all the answers.

That sometimes all you can do is sit down in a dingy bar and clank glasses, watch the people outside walk away with their bags, with their heads down, the winter sky turning from grey to blue, already getting darker.

Work of Hands

I'm taking my ears off again for the television,

buds from headphones shoved into a place where Patti Smith is screaming.

But 2 minutes from a press conference is all I need to hear

about how the world will end. But I'd rather talk about Patti again,

skinnier than a flagpole, shaking her hippie dreads on MTV, belting out

Gloria and People Have the Power.

I didn't know much at 15, but I knew enough to keep

the sound down low the first time I heard her shriek.

Rainy Saturdays when I laid the needle

of her down in my bedroom

set the world inside me spinning.

By the time the bus arrives, I am 16

and there is no 2 hour delay,

no cancellation to keep the glass door of my adolescence

from crashing, from that 9th grade classroom,

called names as if they were curses, as if it were a power

they held over me. I wrote poems to give hell a name,

traded *punk* and *weirdo* for 20 years and a pickup truck,

exhaust and college blowing out into muddy jobsites,

men drinking coffee, running jackhammers,

blasting pop country, the worst music ever invented.

They stand at break and tell black jokes while I stare into a hole

even darker, but I'm new at this.

In the morning, I'll turn off my radio and

go to a place no one wrote a song for yet

where work waits in the freezing rain

in a ditch line, in that dirty boiler room

where a man in a rebel flag bandana

holds a ladder for me, asks if I voted yet.

If I am the leg climbing up,

he is the hand holding on,

my foot on the last rung,

twisted into a place where the pipe always goes in,

where my silence isn't something that has a name,

and we go on like this without talking, doing this work of hands,

speaking to each other in the mute language of the body—

the hunched back, the shaking wrist,

this bearing down and turning,

both of our hands on the pipe

wrenching it down, driving it home.

Beautifully Broken

When you gonna make up your mind?

When you gonna love you as much as I do?

Tori Amos

Reading Between the Lines of an Email to Laurel Garden Apartments, Trying to Get My Security Deposit Back

I want you to know I've cleaned everything.

The walls are how I found them.

I've documented the nicks in the plaster,

the place where the previous tenant threw a chair

at his wife's head.

I've shampooed the carpet the best I could,

left traffic patterns I couldn't do anything with—

crushed piles worn into the path my mother walked

from the sink to the Porta-Potty after surgery.

And I'm sorry about the screen,

we kept it there for her privacy. It had a Chinese silk painting

on the front and heavy legs which leave marks in the carpet wherever it's placed.

There is still a faint smell of smoke on the walls and I'm sorry.

This was from my father, who visited once 20 years after he died,

blew smoke over my shoulder and disappeared like a prayer,

a litany of surgeon general warnings whispering below the threshold

of hearing.

I want you to know I have taken everything out,

the sofa where my niece sat crying after her breakup,

the kitchen table, where I sat, talking her down

from the ledge over the phone till 9 a.m. the next day,

holding the receiver while she slept.

I waited until the sun rose like the bruises that appeared

on her face. Everything's been emptied out.

I'm asking you if it's okay, if you've seen it yet?

Tell me, I haven't left anything behind.

When Your Sister Calls to Tell You She Wrecked the Car on Halloween, or How She Became Medusa

Tonight she won't go out again to pick up takeout and a six-pack

or stop at her ex's to sew bumblebee wings on her daughter

before going out to smoke on a front porch. No celebrity will fix her hair.

15 miles away, you watch Jason and the Argonauts while she

sits in a lawn chair sucking in years of burning air.

She blows out pictures of her kids, a Chevy Blazer's transmission

and whole alimony payments from her mouth like nothing.

No one calls anymore except case managers

and the ghosts that hide behind the paneling.

It's not safe to look at her without risk of turning to stone,

In the scene with the sword, no one realizes Medusa was once beautiful.

She sweeps in, terrible monster, eyes burning.

So you kill her, little by little, dropping money

on the entertainment center for witch potions, tonics for forgetting,

pills for a dreamless sleep to charm the snakes

dancing restless in her mind.

So, back away and watch her from the reflection in the television.

Perseus hesitates with his blade.

Walk backwards like him,

lay the remote down next to her hands.

Top Ten Reasons You Leave Your Sick Kids at Their Grandmother's While Going Black Friday Shopping

1. Because tough love is a room full of secondhand smoke, where your kids can play while your mother chain smokes, cuts coupons, teaches them to breathe in a house full of broken windows.

2. Because the sales today are simply AMAZING.

3. Because Xboxes, iPhones, and Tablets are metaphors for I love you, don't hate me for walking out on you, leaving you with your father, a mortgage, dog-pissed carpets, a bathroom door hanging from its hinges.

4. Because the doorbuster sale at Walmart has Blu-rays for 40 bucks, dirt cheap costume jewelry, tank tops to show off your tanning bed arms.

5. Because you really deserve this adult swim in a sea of cars, the asphalt pool filled with angry shoppers, horn honking and cutting you off for spots.

6. Because the tree in your backyard is dying and you filled the pool with its dead branches, thousands of angry gnats, a hundred tons of dirt because it's just too much to care for.

7. Because when your twelve-year-old got arrested for breaking windows

in abandoned buildings, you became a ghost, an astral form crumpled like a used tissue, and rose from your body, mouth open, dreamless, roaming in a chemical sleep, John the Baptist in faded acid-washed jeans, for 40 years until the messiah came,

a pharmacy tech at the Giant Eagle with your anxiety meds.

8   Because miniskirts and pumps will forgive your sins.

9   Because love means never having to say I fucked up your life permanently. It means *Look at this gold lamé sweater your mother bought for herself.* It means *Doesn't it look good on me?* It means *Honey, I need to hear you say it* and *Now.*

10   Because love means *Quit whining* and *Shut up* on the ride home. It means shutting a door and leaving your mother behind with the engine running, fumbling for knobs for the radio, a wave through a rolled down window, *I'll see you next week,* and *Kisses!*

Still Falling

like the air from a door when it's closing

                        strip of light revealing keys

on a table, crayons, finger paints, glitter on the floor

                        like air in the restaurant between us

I was talking about your children,

                        this strip of life this sudden whatever

like the air this sudden door

                        you kept talking

like the rain

                        from a summer when rice hit your dress

against the door of your car as they drove you

                        away like a door closing

into air before your children came

                        like rain changing over

this sudden whatever

                        I kept talking about children

this weather of you

                        leaving

The Moment

It's like the moment someone reaches for your hand, but stops
short. Like the space between the tree branches, a piece of sky,
blue and visible.
And the wind was throwing things around.
This is how sound travels at night. How light
hits the objects in a room.
A glass bottle, green and fragmented.

You kept talking about
what it would take.

It's like the moment when a bird flies
into a window.
As if air had turned into a wall,
a wall without a window.

It is like the space between the trees,
a light blue and visible.

This is what a hit sounds like.
You kept talking about
leaving, you said he was throwing things around.

And broken light was moving through the space between the trees.

You kept talking about what it would take.

It's like the moment when a phone is thrown

into a window.

As if air had no sound, as if a wall had no window.

It's like the moment someone reaches for your hand

when the light is thrown along the walls of a house,

a light, swirling and blue.

At night the sound travels, and a door opens,

and someone reaches for your arm

and says *Come with us, ma'am,*

and you do.

Visitation

We take our rest

in the car ride over.

Your eyes closed to Haydn,

the slow movement almost reaching

beyond the Lexapro,

and I want to say something

but we've already arrived

at her driveway and five inches of snow.

We drag shovels across the ground

in tandem silence, spot two

city deer nose through the broken pines,

bring inside what's left

of her mail, purge the fridge

of the food past expiration.

And like ruthless movers, we keep going,

caved in boxes full of religious art,

novena beads stapled to cards promising

every desire fulfilled to whomever recites this.

I stack mail next to the olive wood nativity,

Joseph, clad in dust, bending to his son,

the kings holding gifts they can never give.

Everything here bearing witness to this waiting

for a sign, her single panes letting in that frigid air,

that misleading sun flooding her kitchen

with relentless light.

Love Locks

In the car, we share compatible silences and a little Brahms,

the heat that takes ten minutes to get here, and that jacked

up rattle of potholes every few feet. We pull off at the overlook

next to industrial buildings spewing thick plumes from stacks

as we walk past the love locks clicked to the rails of the bridge.

Trump Sucks, Joan Loves Bill, B and V forever scrawled on the steel

in black magic Sharpie. If I finger the loop in your jeans,

pull you closer, it means I'm sorry you hate your job,

I'm sorry the news is on, that the night exploded into gunfire

again, that we start every morning conversation

with *What should we have for dinner?*

The time it takes to stand here together

is the same amount of time it takes to ask a question,

What do we want from our lives? But I keep this to myself, keep reading smudged names as if they're gravestones,

all that looped steel shining from the winter sun,

blinding me for a moment, making me shut my eyes, reach for your hand.

Pest Control

We can't see it, but there's something about the smell—

this chemical sweetness mixed with fear and a *Sorry We've Missed You* sticker left

on our doorknob. Inside, we are sleeping while the silent killer

is busy forcing them out of walls, in between the countertops, the gaps

in the floor tile we picked out together at that home improvement store

over a decade ago. That blue haired tile girl, so helpful,

with so many creative suggestions, Belize, Moroccan Café

and the ever popular Italian, and we forgot where we were

for a moment, that the ceramic felt as dry in our hands as we passed it back

and forth to each other, as if it were a crust of bread we were eating

under an umbrella, the wrinkled, red suns of Paris, or Venice.

But now, it's 2 a.m. and there's a sight that no one plans for.

Small dead beings the size of glitter hanging in air,

husks of dust and loosed stitched cobweb stuck

between laundry room walls.

The smell of wet earth,

and the half shells of flies that have made it

only as far as a cracked window.

This warm summer air that's brought them here as if for some

greater purpose, and we're just too blind to see it.

The Climbers

We leave the world with our heavy clothes on,

slough off a day's worth of sweat and strip dress clothes,

stuck to our skin. Forget the television with its terrible news.

We know that we're too tired for change, except for worn sweaters

and slippers, sharing just enough energy to climb the steps with you

to our bedroom, untwist the question

of floral blankets, cackle together like spinsters, slide off

into this shared body of sleep. After the dream, tomorrow will be rain,

and the city sky will bleed out over the three roofers I watch climb

a neighbor's house, as I walk to work under their downpour

of bent nails, the dust their work stirs up. They toss over empty coffee cups,

ragged shingles, the green one scurrying up with tools,

already knowing the importance of being helpful, too young

to consider the edge, slip of a tennis shoe on wet gutters.

I'm thinking of the first time I fell from a ladder, how the plumber

I worked with said they'd bring flowers if I was dead,

hire someone else the next day.

I learned to survive the white knuckle climb, to hide

shaking knees, and flaming backs, and get there. Leave the boy

on the steep, wet rungs. Don't look back, ask if he's okay.

Let him think about what might happen, the grip this has on his hands,

the rain, when it picks up, how it'll make the decision for him,

air at his back, ground coming up to meet him, the sun shining.

1st Coat

We do it, as they say, for the money.

You transformed in five minutes from business to babushka,

gabardine slacks to a paint specked tee.

I stir color in a five, the faintest coral till it's buttery smooth,

till the dizzy buzz of paint fills our noses and the room

with its slick skin, till the walls sweat with our labor.

Talk soon gives itself away to music,

static radio and the sticky pull as the ceiling is covered,

overlapping the lines I made to the brush's stiff edge.

Each 15 x 20 room we do is a cable bill, each bathroom ceiling

a steak dinner. Every color must be stared at a hundred times,

every drip caught before it falls, and still neither of us

can trust what we see. Like grief, color dries in stages,

thin grey veils of the past disappearing under newer white—

the fading back and forth as we shift on tired legs,

wet rollers in our hands, second guessing whatever we've done,

what we've lost, until we barely feel

when the first pass leaves the wall glistening, then fades true.

We're unsure how it will look in the morning, standing back from

these ghost white walls, satisfied when pistachio green has become porcelain,

amaretto crème. Each color name fills the distant taste of French coffee

in our mouths, the Paris wind on our faces.

We work at it till dark, our faces flecked with semigloss and all that natural light

fading until at last we lose it. Time to hammer those lids down again,

run that water till our brushes are clear.

Spooky Pizza Friday

was what we called it, like a holiday, or good sex,

something that demands a name, leaving you breathless with sweat

and at least one good cigarette.

This is Friday, but even before 7 a.m. we're sending texts,

Can't wait to see you or *Till this is over,* covert as teens or spies

inside the pink bathroom stalls in your office, at a light

changing green, where I'm replying with red lip emoticons

in my pickup to a chorus of horns, middle fingers sticking

out of windows, but instead of go,

I am thinking of a two topping special

and the coupon I left on the desk at home, the 30 minute wait

at night for the passenger seat to get red hot, for the windows to get fogged up

like a first date. But listen, I'm talking about food here, how the swirl of cheese

slumps down the comforters of a spongy crust, pepperoni

burning the cardboard air with the zest of its salt.

I'm driving home from Fellini's Pizza toward the beginning of the story.

where the plot is always based on true events.

The road, freezing, the unforgiving curve, the slick patches I just miss.

I can see my truck flipped over, my head against the dashboard,

cracked windshield, the wheels in midair, still spinning, but this is the Friday

I have enough tread to recover, spin into harmless grass in time

to make it home, the pizza still steaming.

I want to believe it's because we're so tired and deserve the desert island

of our couch, to be envious of our cats again, knitted together like scarves.

Because for two hours, we can forget arthritis, the sister in the hospital,

and walk into televised darkness, follow four unsuspecting coeds

as they get together, then split back up again, set up mics and cameras, say

Make sure you get this, or *Is there a spirit here who wishes to speak?*

They listen for the whispers of phantoms on playback and, just like them,

we are stupidly waiting for the mist of special effects, the deep voice bellowing

Get out into a night darker than the time I was 18 and shaking in my bed,

old enough to tell a shadow or an open closet from the shape of a father

who never came back. No footstep, no banging pipe mistaken for *I miss you,*

You'll get over this.

In the movie, it's the crucial moment of discovery where we are always pausing

for bathroom breaks and another slice, because the story is so bad it's good,

and who wants to see anyone survive it?

The dead jock, the cheerleader panicking in the basement, witnessing

something so terrible no one could possibly believe her. In the end,

the priest never says the right thing. The stained glass shatters into screams,

the evil is always bigger than he is. *Some monsters*, he'll say, *never leave.*

But we don't think about this, we hit play again,

and lean in together, waiting.

The List

We place our clothes on the mattress next to each other,

laid out to keep from wrinkling.

Your dress shirt with the glitter attracting the cat hair and lint,

that working class fallout that settles over everything.

And I can't help but think how much

our empty clothes resemble us,

a little exhausted, rumpled

with the compliance of the well worn, of the machine washable.

Tonight, my hands keep feeling for the dark

of your hands, eyes closed to the extended forecast at eleven.

But what if I added light to this memory?

Poured it through sheer curtains,

held on to it the way yellow does to that empty coffee cup,

lost and sparkling in dishwater,

warm as my hands that rub the stains off of it—

touch the door as I leave, the edge of your thigh.

What if that backyard mimosa rebounds,

grows again next summer,

fills the view of a two lane road,

becomes the wall again of green no one can see past?

It's one a.m. and I keep looking out of the upstairs window

where trees behind our house keep

sashaying like awkward teenagers

or shampoo commercial models,

luxuriant and ridiculous,

as if all they wanted was our attention.

But they turn their backs to us, shake

their chemically treated hair

and a few thousand leaves for us

to rake up every October.

It is summer, a Friday,

and we are sitting in a diner making a list

on a ripped napkin on how to change our lives.

Take an aching back, tuition, a mortgage, and promises,

add to this a glass of wine, the scent of mimosa,

the drive home with the window rolled down,

my hand on your thigh,

every part of yes this is equal to.

Acknowledgements

I'd like to thank *Stone Highway Review, The Open Mouse, Pretty Owl Poetry, The Holiday Café, Ohio Vintage Matchbook Company, Cabildo Quarterly, VerseWrights, Montucky Review, The Fourth River, The Black Napkin, Foundling Review, Right Hand Pointing, Vox Populi, Thirteen Myna Birds, Anti-Heroin Chic, Construction, Dirt Bag Review, Pittsburgh City Paper, Signal Mountain Review,* and *Uppagus*, in which previous versions of some of these poems appeared.

"What the Light Wants," "The Way Back," "The Boy," "The Moment," and "Enough" appeared in *A Room Full of Trees* (Red Bird Chapbooks, 2014).

"The Message" appeared in the e-chapbook *mixtape* (Blast Furnace Press, 2015).

"The Crossing," "Running Storm Pipe Under a Bridge Near Akron, 1997," "Black Angel," "Reading Between the Lines of an Email to Laurel Garden Apartments, Trying to Get My Security Deposit Back," "Top Ten Reasons You Leave Your Sick Kids at Their Grandmother's While Going Black Friday Shopping," "Boy as Girl in Orange Tank Top / How to Eat a Nectarine," "1st Coat," "The List," and "Anesthesia" appeared in the chapbook *The Almost Sound of Snow Falling* (NightBallet Press, 2015).

"Rain" appeared in the anthology *Delirious* (NightBallet Press, 2016).

I'd also like to thank the following individuals for their love, friendship, guidance, encouragement, and inspiring talents, without which this book would not be a reality: David Ades, Jan Beatty, Joan Bauer, Ruth Buckley, Charlie and Judy Brice, Dianne Borsenik, Jay Carson, Rebecca Clever, Judith Dorian, Angele Ellis, Celeste Gainey, Maxine Heller, Jason Irwin, Sheila Kelly, Nathan Kukulski, Nancy Chen Long, Gene Mariani, Sharon McDermott, Leslie Anne Mcilroy, Heather McNaugher, Bob Pajich, Kerridwen Parslow, Richard St. John, Judith Sanders, John Stupp, Arlene Weiner, and Michael Wurster; and my wonderful wife Lynne for her love and inspiration day in and day out.

Robert Walicki's work has appeared in over 40 publications including *The Fourth River*, *Stone Highway Review*, and *Red River Review*. A Pushcart and a Sundress Best of the Net nominee, he currently has two chapbooks published: *A Room Full of Trees* (Red Bird Chapbooks, 2014) and *The Almost Sound of Snow Falling* (NightBallet Press, 2015), which was included in the 2016 Poets House Showcase in NYC. He lives in Verona, PA with his wife Lynne and their cat Buttons.

You can find him at www.facebook.com/robertwalickipoet.

www.ingramcontent.com/pod-product-compliance
Lightning Source LLC
Chambersburg PA
CBHW060533080526
44586CB00012B/721